Marvels of Creation
Sensational Sea Creatures

BUDDY & KAY DAVIS

Marvels of Creation
Sensational Sea Creatures

First Printing, January 2006

Previously published as *Special Wonders of the Sea World.*

ISBN: 0-89051-458-5
Library of Congress: 2005907665

For other great titles visit our website:
www.masterbooks.net

For information regarding author interviews, please contact the publicity department at (870) 438-5288.

PRINTED IN CHINA

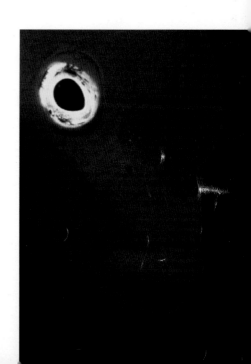

Master
Books
A Division of New Leaf Publishing Group
www.masterbooks.net

Acknowledgments

Writing a book is a team effort, and we have the best team anyone could ask for: the Answers in Genesis staff. Special thanks to Brandon Vallorani and Dan Zordel for their hard work and dedication to this project.

— Buddy & Kay Davis

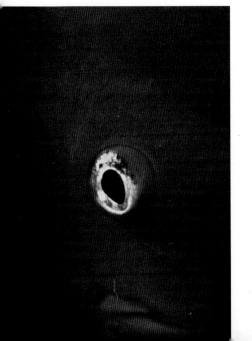

Special thanks to Ian Lauder and Wayne & Karen Brown for use of their photos.

Contents

Introduction

It says in the Bible that God created the sea creatures on day five. In most of the books, films, or programs you see today, God is not even mentioned, but these media are filled with evolutionary theories stated as facts. This book is meant to give God the glory for creating these wonderful creatures of the sea.

This book gives you information on a variety of sea creatures. Each one was specially designed with remarkable features that will amaze you.

The sea contains such a wide collection of different creatures. Some of the animals in this book appear to be very dangerous to man and other animals around it. These features appear as a result of Adam's rebellion in the Garden of Eden. Originally, there would have been no suffering, disease, or death. Sin affected the whole world, and all creation groans because of it (Rom. 8:22). After sin, some of the animals became aggressive and started killing one another. The Bible also tells us that animals began to fear man after the global flood of Noah's day (Gen. 9:2).

God's Word says that there is a time coming when the wolf will lie down with the lamb and the lion will eat straw as an ox (Isa. 11:6–7). In other words, the animals will live peaceably with one another and with man. We look forward to that time.

In the meantime, we will continue to worship God, the Creator of all things and marvel at the special wonders of the sea world.

Barracuda

Twenty species of barracuda are found in deep water in the Mediterranean, western Atlantic, and tropical waters. They are also known both as sea pike (because they are related to freshwater pike) and tigers of the sea (because of their swift attack on prey).

The barracuda is long and slender, with two dorsal fins set well apart. Its body is silver, with darker specks and dark gray-blue stripes down the sides. The tail fin is broad and very strong. The most noticeable feature of the barracuda is its bottom jaw, which protrudes beyond the upper jaw. This shows off both sets of teeth: one row of small razor-like teeth around the outside of its mouth, and a larger set of tearing teeth just inside.

Barracuda are very good hunters, hunting and swimming in small schools. They attack quickly and grab prey with their powerful jaws and sharp teeth. Their eyesight is excellent, even in the muddiest water. The larger barracuda are solitary and may hunt on their own.

The female barracuda lays 5,000–300,000 eggs in the surface waters far offshore. The newly hatched fish begin to hunt immediately. Their food varies with their habitat, but they will eat almost any fish.

Barracuda are popular sport fish because of their powerful runs and leaps. However, they can be poisonous because of the toxins they absorb from their food. Barracuda have also been known to attack fishermen and divers.

Barracuda

PERCIFORMES • SPHYRAENIDAE • SPHYRAENA

LENGTH: Up to 6 feet (1.8 m)
WEIGHT: up to 100 pounds (45.4 kg)
LIFE SPAN: 10–15 years
SPECIAL DESIGN FEATURE: Barracuda have very acute eyesight even in the darkest, muddiest water.
DID YOU KNOW? Years ago, there were reported sightings of barracuda that were 15 feet (4.6 m) long.

Blue Angelfish

There are approximately 80 species of angelfish around the world. At one time it was thought that angelfish and butterfly fish were the same fish. However, there are differences. The most notable difference is the fact that most angelfish are larger than the butterfly fish with a larger spine. They are brightly colored with shades of blue, yellow, black, green, and red.

Angelfish get their name from their pectoral fins. They are located on the back and have a wing-like appearance. Angelfish have a compressed, narrow body shaped like a deep disk. They have scaly dorsal and anal fins. Angelfish are very graceful in their movements although they are very quick and active.

Angelfish are very popular in aquariums because of their shape and beautiful colors. There are some species of angelfish that live in fresh water, and some are marine ocean dwellers.

Angelfish have a very small mouth but it contains many small, crushing teeth. They feed on tiny barnacles, small crabs, and shellfish. They will go after bait that resembles crabs or shellfish, but are seldom caught. Angelfish are edible but they are not sought after as a food source.

Juveniles of some species of angelfish are different in color and pattern than the adults. Adults travel alone or in pairs. They are very territorial and warn other members of their species to stay away.

Blue Angelfish

PERCIFORMES • POMACANTHIDAE
HOLACANTHUS BERMUDENSIS

LENGTH: 24 inches (60 cm)

SPECIAL DESIGN FEATURE: The bright colors of the angelfish warn other species to stay away from their territory. Also, they are very graceful and quick, enabling them to escape predators and defend their home territory.

DID YOU KNOW? Angelfish are the most beautiful and highly colored fish of the reefs.

Bottlenose Dolphin

One of the most loved of the marine animals is the bottlenose dolphin because it is intelligent and social. Dolphins are mammals and must surface to breathe. They live in all temperate zones, and seem to prefer coastal waters on the continental shelf.

The bottlenose dolphin is silver-gray and has a streamlined body designed to swim fast. Dolphins love to hunt and play, and will sometimes jump into the air to look for flocks of sea birds. Though they have good eyesight, dolphins use echolocation to navigate and hunt. With this ability, they hunt fish at any time of day or night. Their diet consists of a variety of fish and crustaceans.

Dolphins swim in pods of a dozen or more animals, sometimes gathering in groups of several hundred. The dolphin's upright dorsal fin is sometimes mistaken for that of a shark; however, it swims and behaves differently than a shark.

Gestation for the dolphin is around 12 months. The calf is about three-and-half feet (1 m) long when born and nurses from its mother for a year.

Dolphins are curious and people-friendly, and seem to enjoy escorting ships at speed. There are many stories and rumors of dolphins helping stranded and drowning people. Unfortunately, dolphins are sometimes caught in fishermen's nets and drown. In captivity, dolphins are trained to perform tricks, and thousands of audiences have enjoyed watching their antics.

Bottlenose Dolphin

CETACEA • DELPHINIDAE • TURSIOPS TRUNCATUS

WEIGHT: 500 pounds (227 kg)

LENGTH: 12 feet (3.9 m)

LIFE SPAN: 50 years

SPECIAL DESIGN FEATURE: Dolphins use echolocation to navigate and find food.

DID YOU KNOW? The dolphin must surface to breathe. They can stay under the water for ten minutes or more.

Butterfly Fish

Called "butterfly" for their small size, bright colors, and darting movements, these fish are thin-bodied with a round shape. They are a variety of colors ranging from yellow with black stripes, white with black stripes, or orange-yellow over black. The markings on the tail resemble those on the head, giving the fish a better chance to evade a predator attacking from the rear.

The butterfly fish has a very small mouth with small, brush-like teeth. Living in warm tropical waters, the fish feed during the day on animal and plant material such as tubeworms and sponges. They also like to bite off the ends of the sea anemone's tentacles; however, the clownfish, which lives in the sea anemone's tentacles, quickly chases the butterfly fish away. After feeding during the day, the butterfly fish will find a secluded place and rest.

Most of the species of butterfly fish can be found around the coral reefs. They usually travel in pairs or a small group over the reefs. It is one of the most popular fish that divers and snorkelers look for when among the reef.

Butterfly Fish

CHAETODONTIDAE• CHAETODON SEDENTARIUS

LENGTH: 6 inches (15 cm)

LIFESPAN: Unknown

SPECIAL DESIGN FEATURE: The markings on the tail of the butterfly fish resemble those on the head, giving the fish a better chance to evade a predator that attacks from the rear.

DID YOU KNOW? There are over 150 species of butterfly fish worldwide.

Clownfish

There are about 300 species of clownfish or damselfish. They live in the western and central Pacific Ocean among the coral reefs, and are especially common in the Australian Great Barrier Reef.

Clownfish are very unique because they are the only fish that can live among the deadly, stinging tentacles of the sea anemone without being killed. A coating of mucus covers the clownfish's body. This mucus is exchanged between the anemone's tentacles and the clownfish's body, resulting in complete protection for the fish.

Although anemones can exist quite happily without their clownfish, it appears that as well as acting as cleaners, these little fish also help, through their fiercely territorial behavior, to protect their host from would-be predators (such as the butterfly fish).

The clownfish actually lures other fish into the anemone and then feeds on the remains. In addition, the clownfish feeds on plankton, algae, and debris from the dead tentacles of its host anemone.

Clownfish live in family groups led by an adult female, which mates with a male from another group. She lays her eggs in batches on a rock near the anemone. The male will guard the eggs, which hatch in four to five days. Sometimes the male will even care for the young until they reach maturity. At that time, they will find their own sea anemone.

Clownfish have both male and female sex organs. When the dominant female dies or is eaten, the dominant male changes into a breeding female to replace her. A juvenile replaces the dominant male.

Clownfish are too small to be hunted for food but are very popular for saltwater aquariums. There is now a restriction on the number of clownfish that can be taken for this purpose.

Clownfish

PERCIFORMES • POMACENTRIDAE
AMPHIPRION PERCULA

LENGTH: 2-1/2 inches (6.4 cm)

LIFE SPAN: 3–5 years in captivity

SPECIAL DESIGN FEATURE: The clownfish live among the sea anemones which kill other fish with their stinging tentacles but do not harm the clownfish.

DID YOU KNOW? The fish are called clownfish because of their bright orange and white markings.

Coelacanth

The history of the coelacanth fish is quite amazing. According to the evolutionary interpretation of the fossil record, this fish dates back to over 380 million years. It died out approximately 80 million years ago at the time of the dinosaurs. No more fossils were found, but in December of 1938, a live coelacanth was caught in South Africa at the mouth of the Chalumna River. It sent such a shock wave in scientific circles that it was named the zoological discovery of the century. More fish were documented between South Africa and Madagascar.

Another Population of coelecanth was found on July 30, 1998, in northern Sulawesi, Indonesia. Biologists learned that this fish has been sold in fresh fish markets in that area all along. The locals even had a name for it — "rajalaut" — which means "king of the sea." The only apparent difference between the African coelacanth called Comoros coelacanth and the Sulawesi Indonesian coelacanth is the color. The African fish is steel blue while the Sulawesi is brown. Scientists now wonder if there are more coelacanths awaiting discovery.

The coelacanth is referred to as a living fossil. When scientists predict evolutionary linage of extinct unknown animals, it is based on their beliefs of the past. The coelacanth was believed to be the ancestor of tetrapods (land-living animals in which human were included). It was thought they lived in shallow water which led their ancestors eventually to take their first step on dry land. Some scientists believed the fins of the coelacanth were primitive first stages of arms and legs. Some biologists thought the coelacanth probably used its fins to crawl along the bottom of the shallow water. Remember, these theories were based only on fossil evidence.

When the living fossil was observed, they were wrong. The coelacanth does not use its fins (which aren't primitive) to crawl along the bottom. It is a swimmer. No way was the coelacanth ready to crawl out on land. It lives in deep water at about 600 feet (200 m). They inhabit overhangs, caves, volcanic islands, and vertical reefs where the water is deep.

The coelacanth is a heavily scaled fish and unusual in that the tail has an extra lobe on the end. It is the only living animal that has an intercranial joint separating its brain and ear from the eye and nasal organs. The unique design allows the fish to lift and move the front part of its head when feeding.

Coelacanth

OSTEICHTHYES • SARCOPTERYGIAN CROSSOPTERYGII, LATIMERIA CHALUMNAE

WEIGHT: up to 200 pounds (90 kg)

LIFE SPAN: unknown

SPECIAL DESIGN FEATURE: The coelacanth is the only living animal that can lift and move the front part of its head when feeding.

DID YOU KNOW? The coelacanth was thought to have died out at the time of the dinosaurs. In 1938, it was found alive and well and was the zoological find of the 20th century.

Cowfish

Cowfish live at or near the bottom of warm, tropical waters all around the world. There are approximately 33 different species of the cowfish. Other names for this fish are boxfish, trunkfish, rock shellfish, cofferfish, and platefish.

The body of the cowfish is enclosed in a six-sided bony plate shell. There are openings for their eyes, mouth, fins, and tail, with a very small gill opening. Their head is conical in shape, sloping down to a very small mouth which is filled with strong crushing teeth. The eyes of the cowfish are large. There are two sharp, forward-pointing spines on its forehead like the horns of a cow. That is where its name comes from.

Because of their unusual shape, cowfish move slowly through the water. The movement of the tail is minimal with most of the swimming motion coming from the dorsal and anal fins as well as the pectoral fins.

The color of the cowfish can differ between male and female. They can be pale green with blue spots or change to yellow with blue spots.

Cowfish live among the coral reefs and actually bite off pieces of the coral. They also eat worms, mollusks, and small crustaceans.

The cowfish lays eggs which hatch in two to three days. The larvae begin to develop their hard shell in about a week. They hide under floating seaweed as they mature. The greatest loss of cowfish occurs when they are eggs, larvae, or young fish. Once they reach maturity, they have a protective armored box and have few enemies. In addition to the armor, some species also give off poison.

The cowfish is considered by some to be a delicacy. It is roasted in its shell and said to be delicious.

Cowfish

TETRAODONTIFORMES • OSTRACIIDAE
LACTOPHRYS QUADRICORNIS

LENGTH: 8 inches (20 cm)

WEIGHT: 2 pounds (0.9 kg)

LIFESPAN: Unknown

SPECIAL DESIGN FEATURE: The cowfish is covered in a bony box like a turtle with holes for their fins, mouth, eyes, and vent.

DID YOU KNOW? Cowfish have two spines in front that look like horns.

Starfish

There are over 2,000 species of starfish found in all the seas. Most of these are found in shallow water, but a few do live in the deep seas. They appear to be most numerous in the northern part of the North Pacific.

The typical body is made up of five arms that radiate from a small central body with a toothless mouth on the underside. The number of arms may vary greatly, as well as the size, from species to species.

The colors of the starfish range from yellow, orange, pink, and red, with a few that are gray, blue, green, or purple.

Plates covered with a thin layer of skin support the body wall of the starfish. Spines also project from the surface singly or in a group. Muscles at their base move each spine. The surface may have little pincer-like jaws mounted on a short stalk on three spines that are positioned close together. They are important in preventing the surface of the starfish from becoming encrusted with algae or other small organisms.

Starfish move by numerous tube feet arranged in rows along the underside of each arm. The muscles of the tube feet propel the starfish along in the water. At the tips of the feet are suction discs, which help secure the starfish to a rock or to its prey.

A starfish has very good regenerative powers and can easily grow back an arm or two if it has lost them. Starfish are carnivorous and feed on fish, crustaceans, worms, and mollusks. There is one species that feeds on coral polyps.

The female starfish releases millions of eggs into the sea. A larva hatches from the egg and from the larva, in about two months time, a young starfish will break free. This is just a very simplified version for one species. There are other species of the starfish that are totally different in their development.

Starfish can be found on most beaches. These starfish are usually dead or dying. They are very popular to collect and are used in decorations.

Starfish

ASTEROIDEA PHANEROZONIA • ARCHASTER TYPICUS

LENGTH: 1/2 inch to 3 feet across
(1 cm–0.9 m)

LIFESPAN: Unknown

SPECIAL DESIGN FEATURE: The starfish can lose one or more of its arms and still survive, and the lost arms will regenerate.

DID YOU KNOW? The starfish typically have 5 arms, but there have been some reported with up to 50 arms.

Sturgeon

The sturgeon is a large bluish-black fish that is very famous for providing caviar. There are a dozen species located in temperate waters in the Northern Hemisphere. The sturgeon spends most of its time in the sea but returns to fresh water to spawn. The largest species of sturgeon, the beluga, lives entirely in fresh water.

The body of the sturgeon is streamlined and scaleless except for large plate-like scutes running from below the gills all the way to the tail. The snout of this fish is very long and broad, with four barbels under its mouth to help locate food. They are bottom feeders so they are constantly stirring up the mud and sand at the bottom. Sturgeons are slow-moving and spend most of their time searching for food.

The taste buds of the sturgeon are on the outside of the mouth. These help in the selection of food. They protrude from a toothless mouth to suck in the food. In fresh water, they eat insect larvae, worms, crayfish, snails, and other small fish. In the sea, their diet consists of mollusks, shrimp, other small crustaceans, worms, and small fish. The sturgeon is a slow feeder and can survive weeks without eating.

In the spring, the female lays two to three million eggs. They hatch in three to seven days and are about one-half inch (1.3 cm) long. The eggs are black in color and very sticky, which adheres them to water plants and stones.

Sturgeons are commercially fished for their meat and oil as well as caviar. They are also caught for what is called isinglass that comes from the swim bladder. This is used for special cements and waterproofing materials, but mainly it is used in clearing white wine.

Sturgeon

CHONDROSTEI • ACIPENSERIDAE
ACIPENSER OXYRHINCHUS

LENGTH: 8 feet, 3 inches (2.5 m)

WEIGHT: up to 1,500 pounds (680 kg)

LIFE SPAN: up to 75 years

SPECIAL DESIGN FEATURE: The sturgeon has four sensitive barbels, slender flaps of skin resembling whiskers, under its mouth, which help locate food under the mud as the sturgeon scrapes the bottom looking for food.

DID YOU KNOW? The sturgeon is well-known as a supplier of caviar. One fish can give up to 400 pounds (181 kg) of caviar.

Triggerfish

The triggerfish live mainly in the tropical coastal waters. Its name is derived from its unusual dorsal locking spine on its back. This spine remains erect until the spine behind it is depressed. When the triggerfish takes refuge and hides in the crevice of a rock, it locks its spine and can't be pulled out.

Looking at it from its side, the triggerfish appears broad and diamond-shaped. Looking from the front, it looks compressed and very thin. When threatened, it can give the illusion of changing from a large fish to a small one by simply changing the direction it's viewed from. About one-third of the triggerfish's body is head. The eyes are fairly large and the mouth is small.

The teeth of the triggerfish consist of eight teeth in each jaw. It feeds on clams, shells of mussels, oysters, crabs, carrion, and many other crustaceans. Its chiseled teeth are used to cut holes in the shells. Some species of triggerfish use their teeth to make sounds by grinding them together.

Triggerfish swim slowly through the water by flapping their dorsal and anal fins. God certainly used His creative genius when He colored the triggerfish. They have an array of bold colors and striking patterns. Some scientists believe they are so colored to ward off predators.

The spine of the triggerfish is thought to stick in the mouth and throat of their predators. Triggerfish can inflict very painful bites to fishermen that handle them. It is believed that these slow-moving fish can defend themselves pretty well. Some species can make sounds by grinding their teeth while others rub together the fin spines. As in all kinds of fish, their sounds are amplified by resonance in their swim bladder.

Some species of the triggerfish are very popular for aquariums such as the clown triggerfish. They are carnivorous so it is best to keep them alone or with larger fish.

Triggerfish

TETRAODONTIFORMES • BALISTIDAE
BALISTES CAPRISCUS

LENGTH: 2 feet long (61 cm)

LIFESPAN: Unknown

SPECIAL DESIGN FEATURE: The dorsal fin on the back of the triggerfish is a locking device. When the triggerfish hides in the crevices, it locks its fin and is almost impossible to dislodge.

DID YOU KNOW? Viewing the broad, diamond-shaped triggerfish sideways makes it appear large. If the fish turns and faces its predators, it becomes as thin as some seaweed.

Walrus

Walrus appear to be timid and quite clumsy, but looks can be deceiving. Walruses will fight to protect their young, and on land they can move as fast as a man can run. They live in colonies in both the northern Atlantic and Pacific Oceans.

The walrus is easy to recognize because of the huge ivory tusks, which are actually canine teeth that grow throughout the entire life of the walrus. The tusks can grow to three feet (91 cm) long in mature bulls and two feet (61 cm) long in the females. They use their tusks while resting by placing them on the edge of the ice, which grips the ice and supports their head. They also use tusks to dig through mud searching for clams and sea snails — the bulk of its diet. They feed on octopus, sea cucumber, cockles, shrimp, and worms.

Tusks are also used to help haul the large walrus body onto the ice and to poke holes in the ice, making air holes for breathing. During the breeding season, the tusks are used against rivals. If angered, walrus have been known to actually spear the side of boats with their tusks.

The adult walrus can weigh over 3,000 pounds (1,361 kg). The fat of a walrus is called blubber and insulates it against the bitter arctic temperatures. The skin on the neck can be three inches (7.6 cm) thick and the fat six inches (15 cm) thick. Their skin is very wrinkled and tough, with deep folds covered with short hair. The color of the walrus is reddish-brown to brown.

The flippers of the walrus are designed to grip the ice on the bottom. They use the front flippers as rudders. The walrus can dive to 275 feet (84 m) for approximately 10 minutes. Normally their dives are about 180 feet (84 m) or less.

The breeding season is from January to March with gestation about 15 months long. The female bears a single young.

The main enemies of the walrus are killer whales and polar bears. Killer whales can cause high mortality, but the polar bears will often ignore the walrus even on land because of its size and thick skin. The walrus is on the endangered species list because man has over-hunted it. There are approximately 250,000 walruses in the Bering Sea.

Since early times the walrus has supplied the Eskimos and the Chuckchee Indians not only with meat but clothing, kayak covering, oil, harnesses for sleds, and blubber.

Walrus

PINNIPEDIA • ODOBENIDAE
ODOBENUS ROSMARUS
LENGTH: 13 feet (3.9 m)
WEIGHT: 3,000 pounds (1,361 kg)
LIFESPAN: 40 years
SPECIAL DESIGN FEATURE: The ivory tusks of the walrus are used as weapons, for digging, and as ice picks.
DID YOU KNOW? The fat or blubber of the walrus is six inches (15 cm) thick and protects it against the frigid arctic cold.

Yellowtailed Snapper

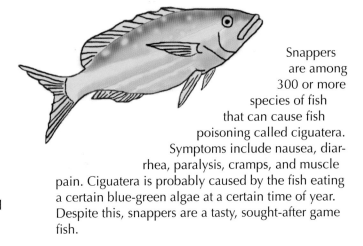

There are 250 species of snappers, with the largest number of them living in the warm Australian seas. The yellowtailed snapper inhabits the shallow warm waters of the coral reefs at a depth of between 20 and 60 feet (10–20 m). They have been found as deep as 400 feet (122 m). The yellowtailed snapper is abundant around the Florida Keys in channels, inlets, and lagoons.

The name snapper comes from their habit of snapping their jaws open and shut when they are landed by a fisherman. The jaws can inflict nasty wounds to careless fishermen. In spite of their small size, they give a good fight and are very popular for that reason.

The yellowtailed snapper has a yellow line which runs along its flank. The tail is bright yellow and deeply forked. The upper side of this fish is blue-gray with a sprinkling of yellow spots. The top of the head is scaleless. They are deep-bodied and have a large head.

The yellowtailed snapper feeds day or night on shrimp, crabs, worms, and smaller fish. They stalk their prey by getting as close as possible. Then they dart out and quickly capture it. On occasion they feed on plant material and garbage from ships.

Little is known about the breeding habits of snappers. It does vary as to the region where the fish live, along with the temperature of the water and the time of year.

Snappers are among 300 or more species of fish that can cause fish poisoning called ciguatera. Symptoms include nausea, diarrhea, paralysis, cramps, and muscle pain. Ciguatera is probably caused by the fish eating a certain blue-green algae at a certain time of year. Despite this, snappers are a tasty, sought-after game fish.

Yellowtailed Snapper

PERCIFORMES • LUTJANIDAE • OCYURUS CHRYSURUS

LENGTH: 12 inches (30 cm)

WEIGHT: 5 pounds (2.3 kg)

LIFESPAN: Unknown

SPECIAL DESIGN FEATURE: Snappers are euryphagous, which simply means they will eat anything. This ability allows them to survive quite successfully.

DID YOU KNOW? The snapper is named because of its many teeth and large jaws which snap open and shut when the fish is caught and pulled on land.

Appendix~
Fish Anatomy

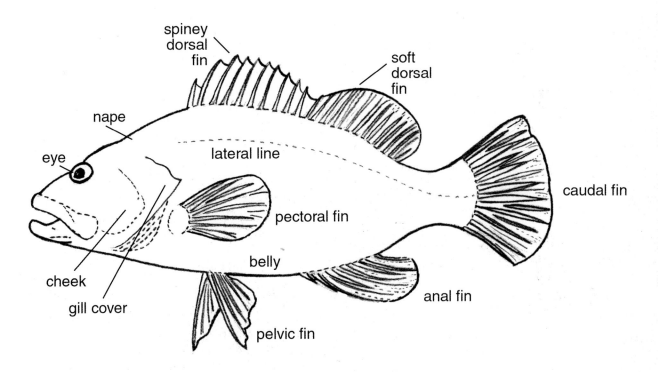

spiney dorsal fin

soft dorsal fin

nape

eye

lateral line

caudal fin

pectoral fin

cheek

belly

gill cover

anal fin

pelvic fin

Intelligent Design

It has been said that scientists know more about the surface of the moon than they do about the sea. New, wonderfully designed creatures lay hidden in the ocean depths, waiting to be discovered. Within the last five years, many new creatures have been found as we pioneer the sea. We can now explore deeper than ever with specially designed submarines. Some of the most bizarre creatures known to man have come to light, such as the luminous anglers of the deep sea. Over 70 percent of the earth's surface is covered by water and it is in this unique environment we've examined some of its inhabitants.

The great variety of sea life clearly shows the creative genius of God. Evolution dissipates into thin air as the complexities of design shine forth. Anyone with an open mind, capable of thinking logically, will come to the conclusion that the hand of the Lord has done this.

Let's explore some of the fascinating design features that glorify God as the author of creation.

Shape

The form of fish fall into four categories. Some are compressed and flattened from side to side, such as the grouper. Flounders, on the other hand, are just the opposite. Their body is flattened from top to bottom to suit their needs as a bottom-hugging fish. Then there are the fish that are streamlined in shaped, such as sharks. Lastly, some have snake-shaped bodies, like eels. Each particular form of the species serves that species of fish for its way of life.

Scales

Most fish are covered with scales. Some are extremely small and thin such as the scales of catfish, eel, trout, and paddlefish. Others are very large and heavy like those on sturgeon or the coelacanth. Scales are an outgrowth of the skin or epidermis. They are like fingernails and are semi-transparent.

The number of scales on a fish remains the same as the fish grows. Scales are arranged in a shingle-like fashion over the body of the fish and serve as protection. There are special cells or glands on the scales that produce the slime for which fish are famous. The slime protects the fish against diseases and fungal infections. This mucus also enables the fish to move through the water without friction. The slippery mucus can help a fish get away when caught by man or beast.

Color

Fish come in a wide, wonderful array of colors. Tropical fish advertise their beauty, and some of them have the most glorious range of colors on earth. Others are dull to blend into their environment. The color of some fish may vary from one geographical range to another and also a change in depth may change color. Some fish can even change colors like a chameleon. In the skin of most fish are pigment cells that produce their color. Scientists have discovered that the pigment cells, or chromatophores, are connected to the nervous systems of some species. Scientists also believe that the eye of the fish is connected by nerves to pigment cells to help the fish blend into its habitat.

The Creator also designed some sea creatures to produce light. Like miniature Christmas lights, the fish glows or twinkles in the dark ocean depths.

Gills

God designed the fish with gills to remove oxygen form the water. Capillaries that lie close to the surface of the gills absorb the oxygen and at the same time expel the waste, carbon dioxide. Fish differ in their ways of breathing — by pumping water through their mouth, by their gill covers, or by swimming through the water.

Hearing

Not long ago, scientists felt that the hearing organs of fish were poorly developed and did not serve much purpose. We now know, because of the invention of the hydrophone, that the sea is full of sound. Fish have only an inner ear. Fish and mammals make sounds by vibrating parts of their body or by grinding their teeth. Fin whales can produce sounds that may have been detected more than 2,000 miles away. Whales and dolphins make a variety of sounds as they communicate with one another. Most fish sounds are grunts, barks, clicks, or growls. Most marine sounds are produced to attract a mate or frighten a potential enemy.

Sight

Fish eyes were designed for underwater vision. The lens of a fish is globular. The lens is rigid and incapable of changing. The lens works similar to that in a camera and moves toward or away from the retina. There is little focal action in the eye because vis-ibility is only about 82 feet (25 m) underwater. Most fish see in color, the exception being the deep-sea dwellers. This is known by the number of color receptor cells located on the retina. Most fish do not have eyelids like mammals because fish eyes are constantly bathed by water.

Bladders

Nearly all fish, with the exception of sharks, mackerels, flounders, and a few others, have a swim bladder which is an air-filled sac under the backbone. This bladder allows the fish to adjust its buoyancy as needed. The fish receives gas into the sac through the blood stream or it can return it.

All of this information that allows these creatures to survive could not have happened by time and chance acting on matter. We haven't scratched the surface concerning the design of fish, having looked at only a few of the 40,000 species.

Origin of Fish

The fossil record is clear. The first time you find a fish in the fossil record, it is 100 percent fish. This isn't what evolutionists would expect if evolution were true. According to evolution, there should be abundant fossil evidence showing the transition from invertebrate to vertebrate. A.S. Romer writes in his book, Vertebrate Paleontology, that the "common ancestor of bony fish groups is unknown." Romer also writes that placoderms pose a deep problem for evolution and that evolution would be better without them. He said that the origin of bony fishes is a "dramatically sudden one."

Glossary

ANAL FIN .... this single fin is found at the rear of the fish.

AXIL...................... the place where the pectoral or ventral fin join the body of the fish.

BAR .... marking on a fish that is vertical.

BELLY .... the underside of the fish body.

BRACKISH .... water that has a mixture of salt-water and freshwater.

BURROW................. a hole in the ground at the bottom made by an animal for shelter and inhabitation.

CAMOUFLAGE............ coloration that blends in with the background or environment.

CARNIVORE.............. something that feeds on other animals.

CARTILAGE............... clear tissue that makes up most of the skeleton on young fish that changes into bone when the fish matures. Cartilage on sharks and rays does not turn into bone.

CAUDAL FIN............. the tail fin.

CAUDAL PEDUNCLE..... the base of the tail of a fish.

CLEANING STATION..... the place on the reef where fish come to be cleaned of parasites by small parasite-eating fish.

CONTINENTAL SHELF ... the bottom of the ocean from the shore to where it drops off quickly.

CREVICE.................. the place in the reef where there is a split or opening where fish can find shelter.

CRUSTACEANS........... invertebrates such as crabs, lobsters, shrimp, etc. which have a hard outer skeleton.

DIURNAL................. something that is active during the day and rests at night.

DORSAL FIN.............. one or more fins that are along the back of the fish.

ESTUARY................. the place where a river or stream flows into the sea.

EURYPHAGOUS........... eating a large variety of foods.

EXTINCT .... something that no longer exists.

FAMILY .... a group that has anatomical similarities.

FINLET .... small fins located behind the dorsal or anal fins.

FORKED .... a tail that is divided into two equal parts.

GAPE .... the place at the rear of the mouth where the upper and lower lip joins.

GILL .... the membrane that serves the fish as lungs, located at each side of the head.

GILL COVER .... the covering of the gills made up of a flap of bones and skin.

HABITAT .... the place where a species lives, grows, and survives.

HERBIVORE .... an animal that eats vegetation most of the time.

INVERTEBRATE .... an animal that does not have a spinal column.

JUVENILE .... a fish in early stages of development that has the appearance of an adult.

LARVA .... the early stage of a fish after it hatches until it reaches the juvenile stage.

LATERAL LINE .... the sensory organ of a fish.

LOBE .... the extension of the tail or fin that is rounded or pointed.

MOLLUSK .... invertebrates such as clams, snails, octopuses, shellfish, and squid where their shell is not segmented.

NAPE .... the area between the eyes and the dorsal fin.

NOCTURNAL .... an animal that is mostly active during the night and resting during the day.

OFFSHORE .... away from the shoreline where the water is very deep.

OMNIVORE .... an animal that eats both meat and vegetables.

OVOVIVIPAROUS .... eggs that remain in the body of the female until they hatch and are born alive.

PECTORAL FIN .... the fin that is located to the rear of the gills

PELVIC FIN .... the same as the ventral fin which is located on the belly of the fish.

PHARYNX .... where the gills are located at the back of the mouth.

PLANKTON .... very small plants and animals that drift in the ocean including jellyfish and very young fish of some species.

POLYPS .... little invertebrate animals that constitute marine growths.

RAY .... the bony support frame of the fins.

SCALES .... semi-transparent plates like fingernails that grow from the skin to cover the fish.

SCAVENGER .... something that feeds on dead animals that it has not killed.

SCHOOL .... a group of fish that travel close together.

SCUTES .... thick scales that form a ridge.

SERRATION .... saw-toothed edge.

SOLITARY .... being, living, or going alone.

SPAWNING .... the discharging of eggs by the female and sperm by the male.

SPECIES .... a group of animals or plants with similar characteristics, capable of interbreeding.

SPINE .... the stiff, sharp-pointed fin support.

SUBSTRATE .... the base on which animals or plants live.

SURGE .... the motion of the sea that makes the waves.

SWIM BLADDER .... a gas-filled sac in the fish that allows it to keep vertical in the water.

TURBID WATER .... water that contains silt and other debris, making visibility very poor.

UNDULATE .... to bend in a wavy motion.

VENTRAL FIN .... same as pelvic fin, which is located on the belly of the fish.

VERTICAL FINS .... includes the dorsal, anal, and tail of the fish.

Bibliography

Ballard, Robert D., Linda Bridge, Sylvia A. Earle, Tee Loftin, Joseph B. MacInnis, Tom Melham, and H. Robert Morrison. The Ocean Realm. Washington DC: National Geographic Society, 1978.

Bisacre, Michael. The Illustrated Encyclopedia of Plants & Animals. The Exeter Books, 1979.

Bright, Michael, editor. The Wildlife Year. Pleasantville, NY: Reader's Digest, 1993.

Burt, William H., and Richard P. Grossenheider. Field Guide to the Mammals. Boston, MA: National Wildlife Federation, Houghton Mifflin Co, 1976.

Burton, Dr. Maurice, and Robert Burton, editors. Funk & Wagnalls Wildlife Encyclopedia, Vol. 1-2-3. New York: B.P.C. Publishing, LTD, 1970.

Carwardine, Mark, and Jim Channell. Explore the World of Amazing Animals. Racine, WI: Western Pub. Company, Inc., 1991.

Cousteau, Jacques. The Ocean World of Jacques Cousteau. England: Angus and Robertson Publishers, 1975.

Doolan, Robert. "The Fish That Got Away? for 70 Million Years." Creation Ex Nihilo, 9(2): 8–11 (March 1987).

Dozier, Thomas A. Dangerous Sea Creatures. Time Life Films, Inc., Publishers, 1976–77.

Dreves, Denis. "Pacific Salmon." Creation Ex Nihilo, 18(3): 26–28 (June–August 1996).

The Kingfisher Illustrated Encyclopedia of Animals. New York: Kingfisher Books, Grisewood & Dempsey, Ltd., 1992.

Legg, Gerald. Zigzag Factfinders Monster Animals. England: Zigzag Publishing, 1997.

Meyer, Angela. "The World of Whales." Creation Ex Nihilo, 19(1): 26–29 (December–February 1997).

Migdalski, Edward C., and George Fichter. The Fresh and Salt Water Fishes of the World. New York: Alfred A. Knopf Publishing, 1976.

Myers, Jack, editor. Nature's Wonderful Family. Columbus, OH: Highlights, 1971.

"Our World." Creation Ex Nihilo, 13(1): 25–26 (December–February 1991).

"Our World." Creation Ex Nihilo, 14(1): 39–41 (December–February 1992).

Parks, Peter. The World You Never See — Underwater Life. New York: Oxford Scientific Films, Rand McNally & Company, 1976.

Peters, David. Giants of Land, Sea & Air — Past & Present. New York: Sierra Club Books, Alfred A. Knopf Publishing, 1986.

Pines, Paula, editor. Nature in America. Pleasantville, NY: Reader's Digest, 1991.

Stokes, F. Joseph. Divers & Snorkelers Guide to the Fishes and Sea Life. Philadelphia, PA: Academy of Natural Science of Philadelphia Publishers,1984.

Vetter, Joachim. "Something Fishy About Lungs." Creation Ex Nihilo, 14(1): 46–47 (December–February 1992).

Wieland, Carl. "Fuzzy Feathers & Walking Whales." Creation Ex Nihilo, 13(1): 48 (December–February 1991).

"Weird & Wonderful Clownfish." Creation Ex Nihilo, 18(2): 32 (March–May 1996).

Wernert, Susan J., editor. North American Wildlife. Pleasantville, NY: Reader's Digest, 1982.

Wexo, John B. Zoobook — Whales. San Diego, CA: Wildlife Educational, Ltd., 1983.

Wildlife Explorer. Stanford, CT: International Masters Publishers AB, 1998.

Wildlife Fact File. Stanford, CT: BV/International Masters Publishing, 1991.